Where Is It?

Written by Asta Thor

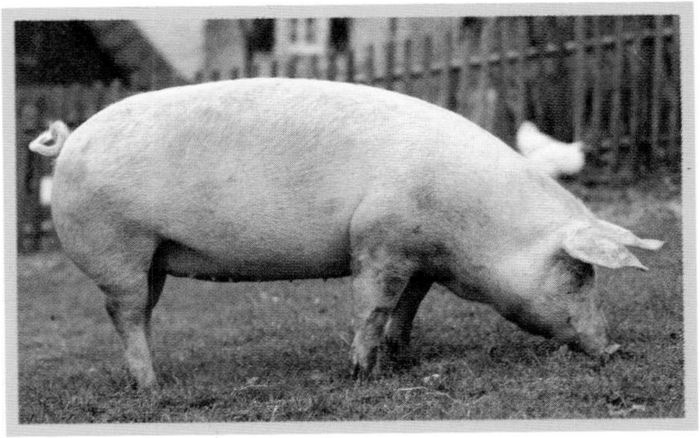

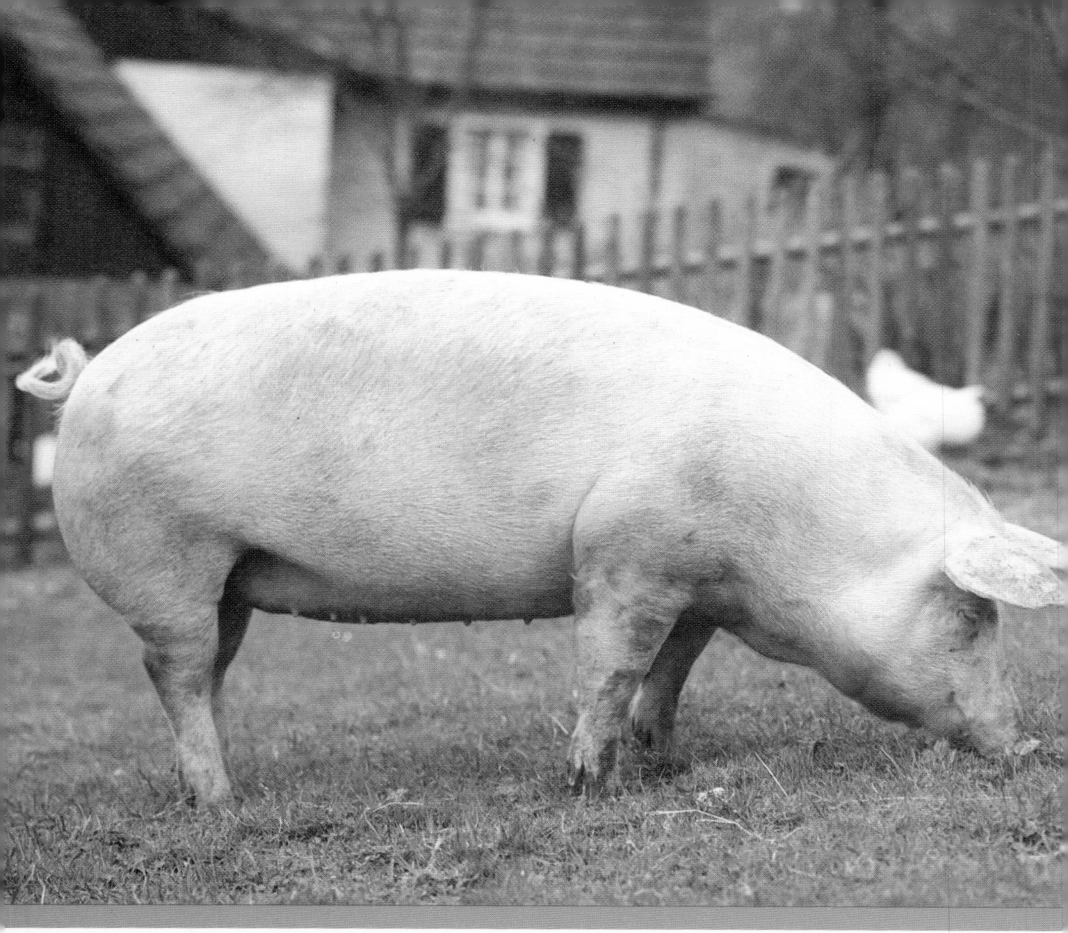

A pig

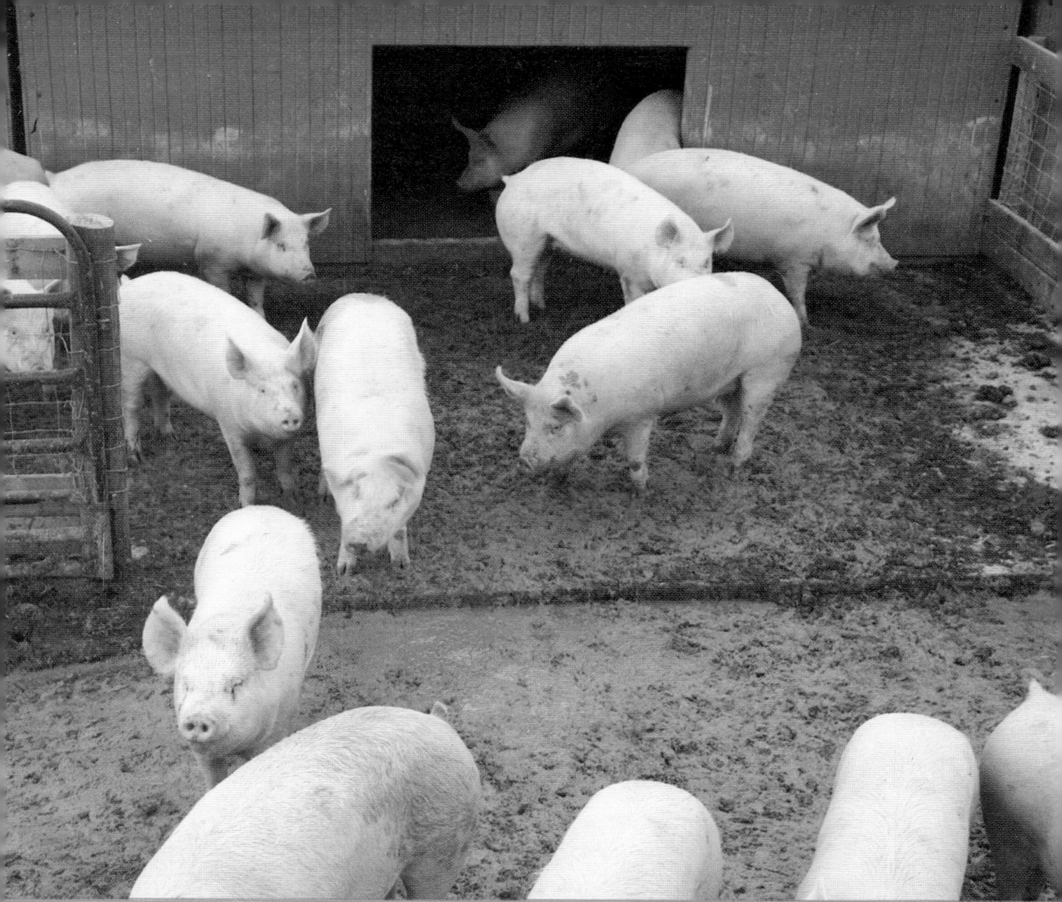

in a pen.

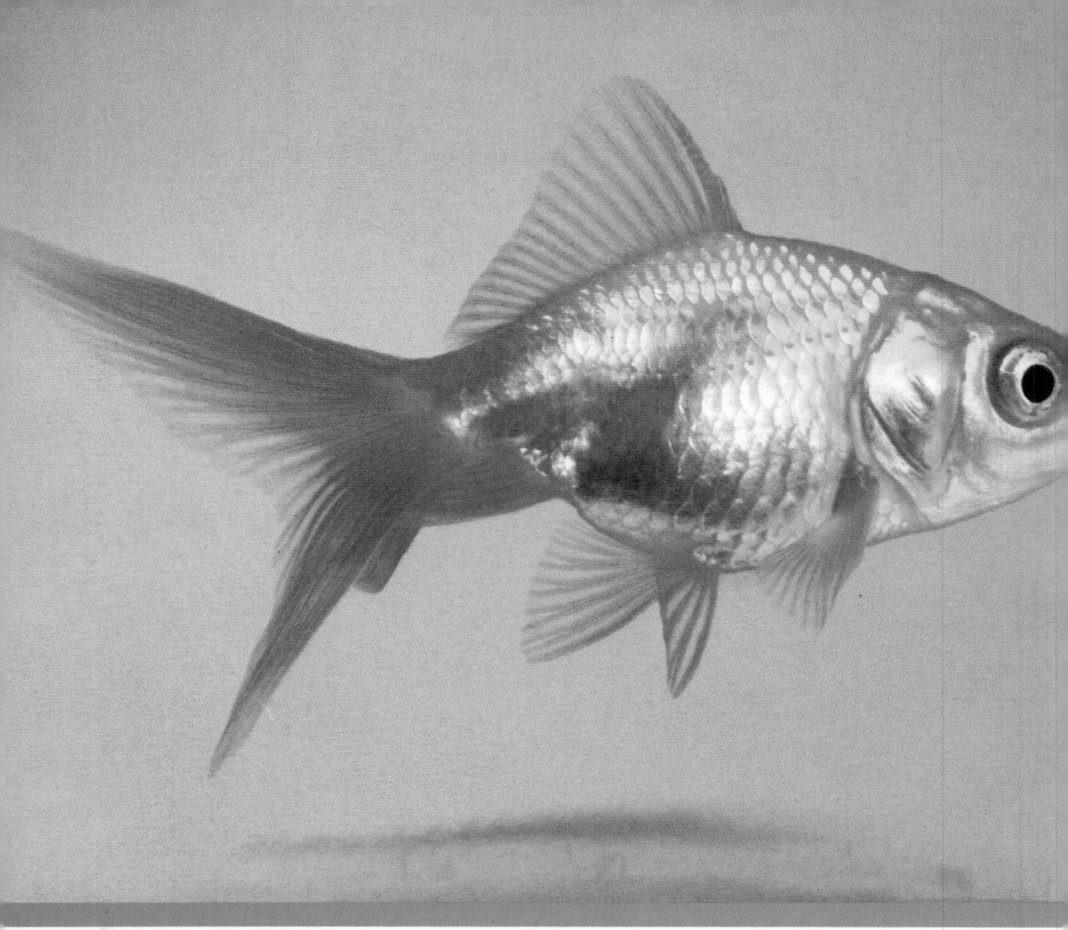

A fish

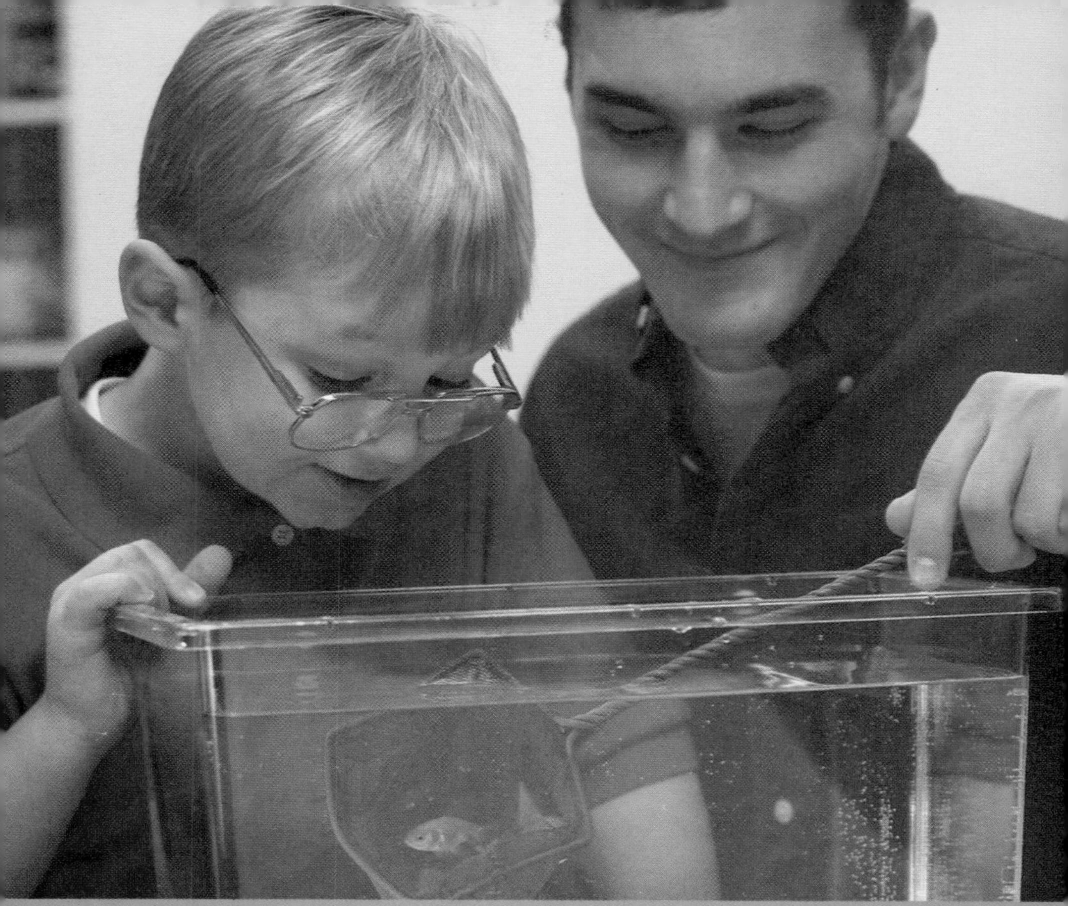

in a net.

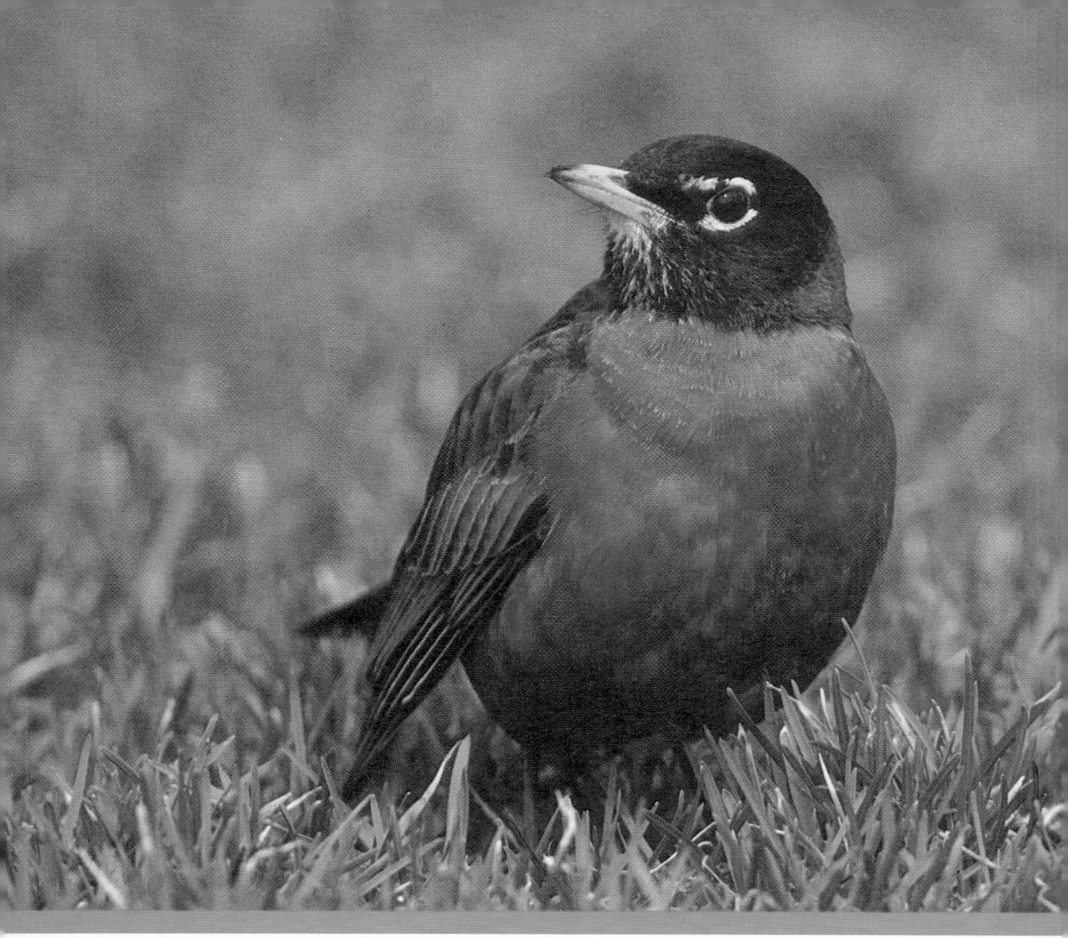

A bird

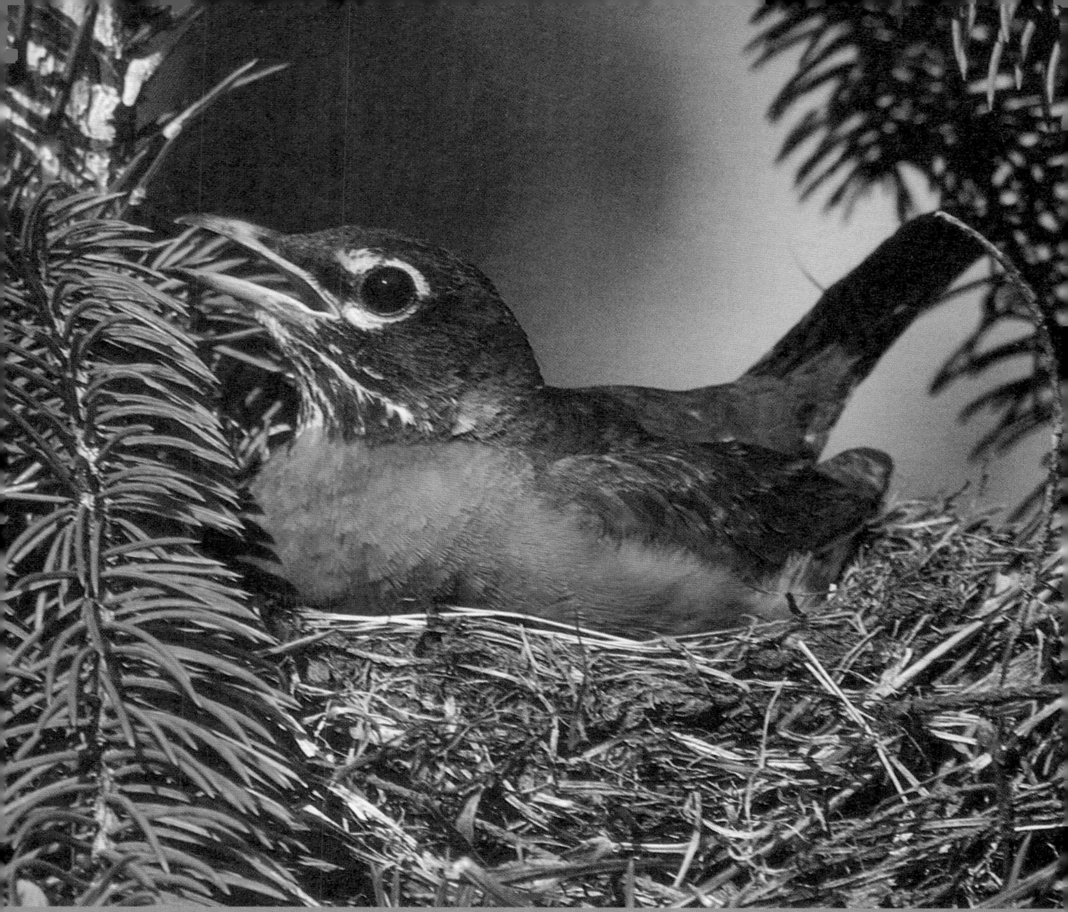

in a nest.

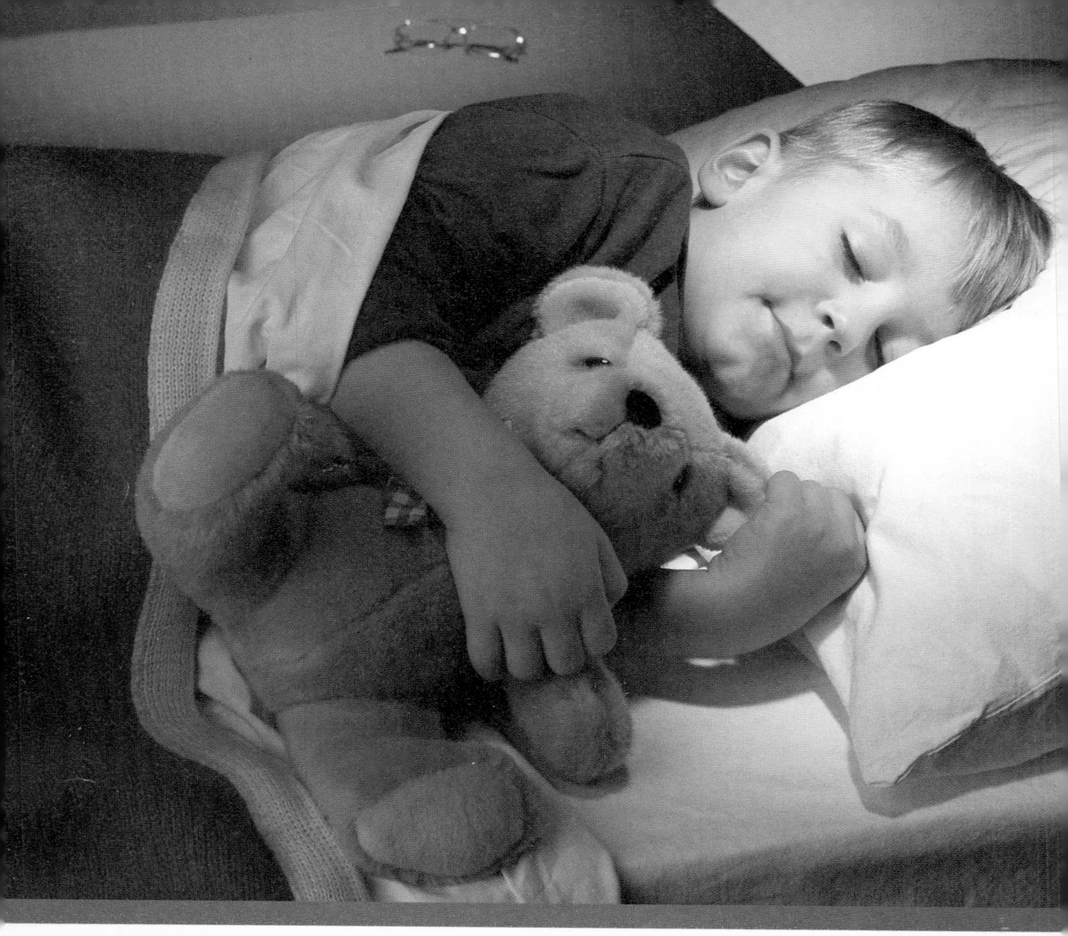

And a bear in a bed.